THE FABRICS
of
MULHOUSE
AND ALSACE
1750-1800

by

ELISABETH ALBRECHT-MATHEY

Conservateur, Musée de L'Impression sur Etoffes, Mulhouse

F. LEWIS, PUBLISHERS, LIMITED

PUBLISHERS BY APPOINTMENT TO THE LATE QUEEN MARY

LEIGH-ON-SEA, ENGLAND

PRINTED AND MADE IN ENGLAND

©
Copyright
F. Lewis, Publishers, Ltd.
The Tithe House
1461 London Road, Leigh-on-Sea
England

SBN 85317 091 6

First published 1968

PRINTED FOR AND ON BEHALF OF THE PUBLISHERS AT THE BLACKFRIARS PRESS LTD., LEICESTER

TABLE OF CONTENTS

ACKNOWLEDGEMENTS

My grateful thanks are due to Monsieur P. R. Schwartz, President of the Musée de l'Impression sur Etoffes de Mulhouse, who provided me with some as yet unpublished documents and was kind enough to read and check both my French text and its translation into English.

Textile Printing at Mulhouse and in Upper Alsace from 1750 to 1800

AT the present time it is impossible to set down with any real degree of accuracy the history of textile printing at Mulhouse, once a small Republic, allied to Switzerland until 1798, and in the Upper Alsace region. Perhaps the full story will be revealed at some future date.

In fact, while a number of people have undertaken studies on the past history of what were once called 'the minor arts' (what nonsense this term is!) it must be admitted that everything touching on the applied arts was disdained for a long period of time and naturally enough, documentary evidence is lacking. There are, of course, many citizens of Mulhouse whether by adoption or origin, who being true lovers of their country have delved into its past history and have undertaken thorough and detailed research into its archives. Thanks to the publication of the results of their endeavours a great many obscure points have been brought into the open. We have attempted in the following lines to provide a synthesis of these publications. Do not be surprised therefore if we have not been able to give you more than a cursory outline of the hopes and fears and disputes in the industry.

Sometimes, unfortunately, we cannot provide more than a mere list of names unearthed. A considerable amount of research through archives will still be necessary to clear up certain obscure matters and this will necessitate years of work.

In the area bounded by the Vosges Mountains the River Rhine and the Jura Mountains, the cradle of textile printing is situated at Mulhouse. It was on the 3rd of December 1746 that J. J. Schmaltzer, Samuel Koechlin, Jean-Henri Dollfus and J. J. Feer bought a house and bleaching establishment in Mulhouse at Fritschmanngasse (now the Rue de la Loi) and a second bleachery, Porte-Haute, sited alongside a small stream, the Steinbächlein. The official name for this new enterprise for textile printing first saw the light of day on the 24th February 1747 as: 'Koechlin, Schmaltzer et Cie'.

Two questions should now be asked:

Who were these four gentlemen who embarked on this new venture in textile printing?

How did they first conceive the idea of founding their manufactory, the first-born of a whole cluster of others, all more or less famous, and more or less lasting in time, but all of which contributed to the renown and the present character of our dear City of Mulhouse.

Mr. R. P. Schwartz, President of the Mulhouse Textile printing museum, published a study in the *Bulletin de la Société Industrielle de Mulhouse* in 1950/1951 (see Bibliography) entitled 'Beginnings of calico printing at Mulhouse'. This was based on documents filed away in the archives and provides great help in answering some of our questions.

The Basle trading house known as *Veuve Emmanuel Ryhiner Aîné et Cie* had also white Indian cotton printed at Amsterdam and sent its employees along to supervise all the various methods and operations involved in printing[1]. From being an observer, Samuel Ryhiner (1696–1757) became a man of action in this field as soon as he returned to Basle from

1. *See note 1, page 31.*

Amsterdam; in 1716–1717 he set up several printing tables in Basle. The new industry quickly flourished, became self supporting and grew to such an extent that it produced an offshoot in 1738. Its products were sold mostly in Lorraine, at Strasbourg and Francfort.

In France this trade was prohibited at the time. Under pressure from the silk merchants and cloth manufacturers a number of Royal decrees and edicts, some 80 of the former, were issued between the 26th October 1686 and the 30th June 1742.

Here is an extract from an Order dated 26.10.1686 (National Archives – F 12 1403): 'His Majesty in Council ordains that from today all manufactories in the Kingdom engaged in the painting of white cotton cloth shall be closed and the moulds used in their printing be destroyed. His Majesty expressly forbids their re-establishment and forbids his subjects to paint the said cloths, the engravers to make any moulds for the said printing under pain of confiscation of the products, moulds and all other utensils, plus a fine of 3,000 *livres* per head immediately, of which one third shall be paid to the informer, one third to the hospices of the region and one third to the farmer general'.

On the 1st of January 1688 an order was issued forbidding the purchase or sale of any painted fabrics.

Denunciations and searches proceeded apace. The punishments meted out were often severe: fines, withdrawal of masterships from seamstresses and tapestry makers, imprisonment, whipping, even a sentence to the galleys for some of the smugglers involved.

In 1720, following an outbreak of plague at Marseilles and Aix, which was introduced by several cases of contraband goods from the ship 'Grand St. Antoine', a draconian decree was issued on October 11th: 'It is forbidden under pain of death to introduce in the Kingdom any fabrics from the Indies, China or the Levant, or any fabrics made in the City of Marseilles'. (Marseilles had been a free port since 1669).

On the 5th June and 17th November 1722, two Orders renewed the prohibitions and authorised the employees of the local tax gatherer to undertake house to house searches under the aegis of the salt granary of Troyes for the purpose of seeking out spurious salt as much as for uncovering printed cloth. The orders were renewed in identical form on 5.7.1723, 14.12.1723, 9.5.1724, October 1726, 28.1.1727, 15.4.1727 and 30.11.1730.

During this entire period the manufacture of printed calico was authorised at Mulhouse, a small independent Republic, an ally of Switzerland and a foreign enclave on French soil. For customs purposes, Alsace remained a separate region even after having joined the French Crown in (Westphalian peace) 1648. Trade in chintz is legal, even if its manufacture is not. It watched its neighbours in nearby Basle.

What was the actual situation reigning in Mulhouse before 1745 in the view of the Basle manufacturer Jean Ryhiner's manuscript on cotton printing dated from 1766 (Bulletin de la Ste Industrielle. III 1950.)? – the Lorraine markets, principal clients for Basle's exports, never had enough goods to sell since demand is far in excess of Basle's manufacturing capacity.

In Basle itself, calico printing is a profitable industry, but it is undertaken by only two manufactories, which were disinclined to expand their production lines since they wished to operate entirely on their own resources in matters of capital.

Mulhouse itself lay astride the main route from Lorraine to Basle. (The Duchy of Lorraine, which lay outside the French frontier at that time, was then the great source of supply to the Kingdom in contraband chintz). This route was the one taken by the Lorraine salt waggons on their way to the south of the country and towards Switzerland, which country imported wine from Alsace. It was therefore in continuous contact with the traders of Lorraine who provided a stream of useful information.

The moneylenders of Mulhouse granted a better rate of interest of 5% and 6%, against less than 3% at Basle.

There were a large number of fields so necessary to bleaching and drying operations. The climate was relatively one of clear skies and sunshine. A plan of the city in 1797 shows that the site was bounded by two rivers, the Steinbächlein and the Ill.

Finally, there was the human factor to be considered: the city had a hard-working and enterprising population which, in local terms, had no great economic resources to fall back on. These conditions were enough for a small group of men to decide on the erection of a manufactory. We have already given their names. Now let us take a closer look at them: J. J. Schmaltzer (1721–1797) very probably a wholesaler in the trade; in any event, he was a member of the Tailors' 'Tribe' on whose books he was entered as a 'Merchant' (Kaufmann)[2].

Samuel Koechlin (1719–1776) also registered as a 'merchant' in the Tailors' 'Tribe'.

J. H. Dollfus (1724–1802), an artisan painter, registered thus with the 'Tribe' of Blacksmiths.

J. J. Feer (1715–1780) possibly a wholesaler and merchant, also registered with the Tailors' 'Tribe', but with no further details.

These four young men, aged 24, 25, 27 and 31 years respectively, do not look like past masters in the trade. Thus they were obliged to require the assistance of the two 'manu-facturers' (Fabriquants in French). These were Henri-Paul Desplands, a Protestant refugee from Anduze in the Languedoc whose father had settled in Geneva (Switzerland) and his brother-in-law, Jean-Pierre Bonne, also of Geneva, but a native of Challex in the French neighbourhood of Geneva.

Henri-Paul Desplands had been a designer and engraver and since at least 1736 the co-owner of a printing Manufactory at Port de Cressier (between Neuchâtel and Bienne).

Jean-Pierre Bonne was most probably a printer, since 1738 at least. (On the 14th April 1738 he married Marguerite-Dorothée Desplands). The two brothers-in-law were obliged to leave their manufactory (closing down?) for reasons unknown during the winter of 1746–1747.

The undertaking began output prior to June 1747, on a seasonal basis as all the printing factories in Europe at that time, it was then impossible to wash and dry the goods in the fields in winter. A temporary exemption of duties was granted to them on the 28th of June and 5th July 1747. These taxes (Pfundzoll) were in fact a tax levied by the city on all goods sold in Mulhouse.

This went on for five years. In 1752, a second manufactory appeared in Mulhouse and its emergence created a problem for the municipal authorities. It was called Hartmann et Cie. and had three associates:

Hans-Michel Hartmann (1726–1802) son of a deceased weaver in the wool trade.

Jean Dollfus-Mieg (1729–1800) an apothecary and holder of one of the three dispensaries of the town.

Mathias Schmerber (married in 1745) dyer in both fast and non-resistant colours (these are from dye-woods, whereas fast colouring uses madder). Mathias Schmerber, through his trade, was therefore a member of the Dyers' Corporation expanding from the Tailors 'Tribe' which had very strict rules. As soon as he attempted to step out of line his colleagues brought a suit against him: this happened when he wanted to buy and install a boiler away from his residence.

In 1752, agreement was reached between Koechlin, Schmaltzer & Cie., and Hartmann & Cie, for a division of work on certain types of goods. Such an agreement is very valuable in itself, but it is essential that there should be no dispute between the parties concerned. Unfortunately, this was not long in coming about, and numerous problems were raised concerning this new profession which took in design, engraving, dyeing and trading proper. Is Schmaltzer a trader and can he, in his own particular trade, bring suit as such? Can a calico printing manufactory have workshops both inside and outside the city walls, a feature forbidden to artisans? What is the position of a dyer who enters into partnership? It was left to the authorities to solve the problems. From the year 1753, thanks to the fact that these disputes all helped to clear the air, calico printing was recognised as a 'Free Art' in Mulhouse. The equivocal position of the new industry was thus finally settled in the most favourable way for its greater good, even though it had already enjoyed six peaceful years of work.

What could have been the importance of the first Mulhouse Indiennes factory and the qualities produced? We had to wait till 1949, when a very important document was fortuitously discovered in the municipal archives, where it had not been inventoried. It is a request concerning the taxation of this new enterprise, considered to be too high, and accompanied by a monthly enumeration of the sales amounting for the year 1749 to 97,324 *livres* tournois, goods totalizing 3,014 *livres* tournois having been returned. Amongst the latter we find 'Calanca' and 'ordinary Indiennes'. This means that in the third year of its existence the manufactory produced not only current ware but also qualities of a high standard, with many colours, a Calanca being similar to the Indian Kalemkar from which it took its name. The prices being about 40 *livres* tournois the piece for the Calanca and about 21 *livres* tournois, for the Indiennes ordinaires we have a turnover of about 100,000 *livres* tournois to extreme possibilities for a yearly production: 2,500 pieces of Calanca or 4,800 pieces of ordinary Chintz with one colour of 15/16 aunes de Paris of a width of 3/4.

According to the detailed production figures given in 1766 by the Basle manufacturer Jean Ryhiner, for a table working only 36 weeks a year (on account of the bad weather prevailing in winter), the 4,800 pieces of ordinary chintz could have been made with 5 to 6 tables[3] and 15 to 20 persons (each table having its printer accompanied by his boy). The Calanca could have necessitated about 10 tables, it depending on the number of colours wanted. (We exclude from the operatives the pencilling maids).

It is not known if the manufactory made also blue and white goods, by the so-called resist system in the indigo vat. It had always to quarrel with the Corporation of the Dyers in blue, and when J. J. FEER took an interest in the Sierentz factory (see later) he wrote (1763) to the Mulhouse authorities that he 'could make there also blue qualities, so called Porcelaine, which are not produced here'. In 1764 the Mulhouse production seems to have been ordinary chintz, small and large Patnas Calancas, ordinary handkerchiefs, handkerchiefs with red, black and blue, fine qualities illuminated, also with 2 or 3 reds. It can be supposed that the blue of the handkerchiefs had been pencilled in with pencil-blue, as we know that this sort of blue was already known in Mulhouse, having been sold in 1760 to a manufacturer of this town by a Basle druggist and colour-maker. According to the above quoted Jean RYHINER, the Patnas were the battle-horse of the Mulhouse printers towards 1766. (Faced with a shortage of domestic staff caused by the recruitment of pencilling girls a new regulation was promulgated on the 4th of May 1764, laying down the conditions under which female labour, aged 15 years maximum, could be employed, unless the women concerned were in a frail state of health.).

In 1758, after 12 years of operation, the initial manufactory Koechlin, Schmaltzer & Cie split up into four new undertakings:

'Koechlin Dollfus & Cie' headed by Samuel Koechlin until 1771. At that date he was replaced by his son Jean.

'Schmaltzer & Cornetz' (the latter was the father-in-law of the former). J. J. Schmaltzer headed this enterprise.

'Feer & Huguenin', directed by J. J. Feer.

and lastly, 'Frères Dollfus, Vetter & Cie', directed by Jean-Henri Dollfus.

Jean Koechlin died in 1781. The manufactory continued in business with the partners who were left in the name of 'Frères Koechlin' and became "Koechlin & Cie" in 1797.

In 1800, Nicolas, the son of Jean Koechlin, took over the manufactory.

Schmaltzer & Cornetz became in 1772: 'Schmaltzer & Mieg' on the arrival on the scene of Mathias Mieg. In 1775, the enterprise took on a less formal note under the name of 'Jean-Jacques Schmaltzer', being a family enterprise consisting of Jean-Jacques Schmaltzer Senior, J. J., and Pierre, his sons, and Josué Risler, his son-in-law. In 1776, J. J. Schmaltzer Senior left the manufactory to lay the foundations of a new printing works at Munster. (Not far from Colmar, Upper Alsace).

During this time, the 'J. J. Schmaltzer' Company, founded in 1775, continued its work at Mulhouse as mentioned above until the year 1786. Then Jean-Jacques Schmaltzer Junior left the family business in order to found a new one: 'Jean-Jacques Schmaltzer Fils Aîné' with Jacques Laederich in temporary partnership. In September 1789, the business went bankrupt and ceased trading.

'Feer & Huguenin' – In the archives of the City of Mulhouse we find a deed of sale dated 19th September 1758 for a piece of land at the 'Schlittweg' in Mulhouse, signed by J. J. Feer and Huguenin, manufacturers of printed calicoes. On the 31st of March 1759 a contract was drawn up between J. J. Feer and the brothers Daniel and Henri Huguenin. But at some stage between 1762 and 1764, there were disagreements between the partners and the contract was broken. In December 1764, J. J. Feer went into partnership with Frederic Cornetz the Younger, a bleacher. During this time, and while he was still in partnership with the Huguenin brothers, though only a short period of this association remained to run, J. J. Feer had dealings with Antoine Baumgartner of the Maison Bian at Sierentz (which was located some 15 kilometres south-east of Mulhouse). Joseph-Jérôme Bian and Steffan, a former Burgomaster of Sainte-Marie-Aux-Mines (Upper Alsace) asked the Baron de Lucé, the Provincial Administrator of Alsace, for a grant of exclusivity in the year 1756 for the setting up of several hand spinning mills for cotton products in Upper and Lower Alsace, and also for permission to bring in foreign weavers to work on cotton and linen and to teach weaving. They were granted the monopoly of this trade and received formal authorisation to proceed on the 29th of March 1756.

J. J. Feer signed the following agreement.

'An agreement for the manufacture of chintz at the manufactory situated at Sierentz between Messrs. J. J. Feer and Antoine Baumgartner, both of Mulhouse.

Mr. Baumgartner who exploits and operates the said manufactory both for his own account and for that of Messrs. Bian & Cie, the proprietors thereof, having considered that it would be to their advantage to have also a textile printing works, believe that this would make it easier to dispose of their products than merely selling them in the raw state.'

In partnership with Mr. Feer, who would provide the necessary funds for this new establishment for the production of 'porcelaines', *Finschitz*, *Cubschitz*, 'peruvians', fine crimson dyed grounds⁴ and similar articles, either on their own cloth or on that purchased from outside, especially fine cloth from Toggenbourg and Zurich, – and so that Messrs. Bian & Cie shall not incur any risks in case the venture is not a success, it is also agreed that Mr. Farnet, taken on by Mr. Feer as 'fabriquant' and wholesaler, shall work the said fabrics at his own expense and for the prices paid in the County of Neuchâtel and at Mulhouse, and in case our funds prove insufficient for him to purchase the required number of pieces, he shall be allowed, in order to keep his workers busy, to take work on a commission basis and to print cloth for his own account, always providing that the work he carries out for us is not delayed thereby, and also promising to use only old designs for others, and the new ones solely for our account, – and it is also understood that in the trade as in the two manufactories concerned in the conversion of cloth into chintz, Mr. Farnet will act as much in his own name as for Mr. Feer, and also assisting Mr. Baumgartner in every way possible to procure the greatest good for the Company.

In pursuance of which Mr. Feer will draw profits and interest on his capital to the same amount as Messrs. Bian & Cie and will ensure that the books are kept in two entries so that accounts are clear and accurate.

This agreement will be furnished to Messrs. Bian & Cie when the inventory, which Mr. Baumgartner is preparing, is legalised and approved by those concerned, and, should they themselves disagree with the union of the two manufactories, Messrs. Feer and Farnet shall be allowed to withdraw their capital in terms of printed goods, tools and utensils and all that depends thereon, and Messrs. Bian & Cie shall keep all that which belongs to the manufacture of untreated fabrics, it being understood that an equable apportionment of the balance shall be arrived at, and that Messrs. Feer and Farnet shall have six months in which to withdraw, set up elsewhere and liquidate the matter.

Signed in two copies at Sierentz, 1.Xbre 1763.

     J. J. Feer   Baumgartner   Farnet.'

To sum up, J. J. Feer was only interested in producing qualities which were clearly defined in advance. To this end, he promised:

   to supply all the necessary capital,

   to look after the accounts,

to employ a technician, probably from French Switzerland, who would do the printing work for him at Neuchâtel and Mulhouse rates, materials from Bian & Cie, as well as other work, of high quality purchased in Switzerland,

to undertake the business risks involved. If he was not able to provide Farnet's tables with enough work at the time, then the latter could take on work for others.

---

4. *See note 4, page 32.*

Unfortunately, J. J. Feer's agreement is post-dated (1.X.bre 1763) and he soon learns that Baumgartner has undertaken certain large deals on credit, paying 6,000 *livres* tournois for Swiss fabric with another quite different idea in mind, and also that Farnet had taken on too many workers in what was a season that proved to be a bad one. Little by little, the juridical situation of the various parties to the agreement became completely entangled. A court case followed, ending in the year 1765. But for all that, J. J. Feer's idea was an excellent one. With better collaborators, he might have succeeded in setting up at Sierentz the first enterprise of its kind in Upper Alsace, taking in weaving and printing under the same roof. Such a degree of integration would have been impossible at Mulhouse where the weavers, with the support and encouragement of the authorities, adopted a much too individualistic stand. What was the fate of the manufactory after 1765? Its fate is not yet known, even though Jean Ryhiner, the calico printer of Basle, said in 1766 that 'the Sierentz manufactory had the best indigo cold vat in the region and appeared to be in the forefront in the technical sense. Ch. Schmidt in his work of 1912 '*Une Conquête Douanière*' avers that a manufactory of Sierentz was bought by Robert and Garnier from Bar-le-Duc, and later left by them to their chief salesman, one Zeller.

From another source, the Documentary History of the Industry at Mulhouse, we learn that in April 1771, Baron de Waldner, Lord of Sierentz, wrote to Trudaine, Comptroller-General of Finance, that he had spent a small fortune in setting up two manufactories in the burgh; one for painted fabrics, and one for 'porcelaine' pipeclay and earthenware. We have no means of knowing if this was a true manufactory of porcelaine proper, or whether it refers to the process known as 'porcelaine' used for dyeing indigo with a kaolin *réservage* (resist) to make blue and white articles.

However, in 1772, Baron de Waldner informs Mr. d'Aigrefeuille, Inspector of Manufactories in Alsace, of the difficulties which he experienced with the printed goods from his Seigneurie at Sierentz. On 23rd of June 1772, Mr. d'Aigrefeuille wrote to the Abbé Terray, then in charge of the Royal Treasury and all matters related thereto, the Directorate of all taxation matters under Louis XV, the Clergy, Internal Trade and External (excluding by sea) Trade of the Kingdom. . .

In his reply, the Abbé Terray stated that he desired more details on the subject of the painted cloth of the Upper Alsace region and sent a questionnaire for completion. In his answering letter, Mr. d'Aigrefeuille went into a mass of details of a technical nature concerning the manufactories of Sierentz, Saint-Marie-aux-Mines and Wesserling, the latter being the most important of the three in 1765, but unhappily closed down temporarily in 1772.

Mr. d'Aigrefeuille's answers to the questionnaire are given below as regards the manufactory at Sierentz:

'*Number of master craftsmen and apprentices:*

The Sierentz manufactory employs in the printing works: 40 journeymen printers, 40 apprentices, 1 master dyer and 2 assistants, 2 master designers, 5 engravers, 3 apprentice engravers, 8 satiners, 6 calenderers-launderers, 1 master craftsman, 15 assistants, 150 girls for pencilling work, washers, beaters and labourers 20.

For certain qualities of specially made cotton cloth (façonné) sold in small quantities to small merchants or pedlars: 22 master craftsmen, weavers, with spinning girls for work with hemp, linen and cotton 500, reelers 35.

'*Cost of Labour:*

All workers in the manufactory are paid weekly; the journeyman printers 9 and 10 *livres* per week, the apprentices 4 *livres*, the master colourist 24, the assistants 4 *livres* 10 *sols* each, the master designers 15, the engravers 12, the apprentices 6, the satiners 6, the calenderers 5, launderers 6 *livres* 10 *sols*, each assistant 4 *livres* 10 *sols*, each girl 3, washers, beaters, labourers 4 each.

Fabric works are paid piecework and earn: master weavers 9 *livres* and 15 sols per 30 *aunes* piece, spinning-girls at 20 *sols* per piece up to 45 *sols*, wind-reelers 3 *sols* per pound of thread.

Quantity, quality and price of different materials used:

The Sierentz manufactory has an output of 20–22,000 pieces per annum of printed cloth for which it needs 15,000 pieces of fine Swiss cloth at 21 *livres* per piece bought locally. Overheads must be added to this, 7 *livres* 9 *sols* per quintal weight.

3,000 pieces of ordinary Swiss cloth at 15 *livres* local bought and costs of 7 *livres* 9 *sols* per quintal weight; 259 tons of indigo from San Domingo at 700 *livres* the quintal; 2 *livres* 14 *sols* costs per quintal at Basle; 360 quintals of madder from Holland at Basle, 120 *livres* the quintal, costs per quintal 18 *sols;* 120 quintals of senegal gum and gum arabic at Basle 192 *livres* per quintal, costs 18 *livres* per quintal; 60 quintals of nut-gall from Aleppo at 75 *livres* the quintal at Basle, costs 18 *livres* the quintal.

Also different ingredients such as alum, Cyprus, vitriol, Saturn salt, nitrate, ammonia, arsenic, totalling 25,000 *livres* at Basle. For the small types of specially made fabrics (Façonné); 60 quintals of cotton at 110 *livres* the quintal up to 160 the quintal at Basle; 12 quintals of linen at 95 *livres* and 10 quintals of hemp at 60 *livres* the quintal.

Different methods employed, and machines used which are worthy of note:

The most common method is the one in use for crude cloth at the Sierentz manufactory at its beginning then in competition with the Swiss. With a view to decreasing labour costs, a 500-bobbin unwinding machine was installed, this being copied by the Swiss also.

Quality and costs of articles manufactured:

The Sierentz manufactory prints up to 22,000 items of ordinary type: *Patener, mi patener, Suratter, Pulvinater, mi-calancar,* blue ground, green and yellow grounds, *schütz, coups-schütz, Peruviener, Porcelainer* and *Toiles d'Orange*[5]. All these different sold for 18 *livres* per piece of 15 *aunes* up to a maximum of 48 *livres.*

The manufactory produces 'Siamese' and 'Paris' fabrics, fustian and coarse calico; 12,000 pieces per annum which it sells per 30 *aunes*, from 60 to 95 *livres* each.

Markets:

Alsace and Lorraine.

Method of transport:

By waggons.

Comparison of production this year with the previous year:

Manufacture generally is down by one-third, which gives an idea of the losses which must follow in the next season.

Other general points relating to the manufacture in-so-far as they are progressing or declining:

The entrepreneurs and owners of the Sierentz manufactory have made known that Swiss competition[6] has destroyed the advantages they drew from their trade both for themselves and for their country. They have shown how the foreigners have taken over a most important industry, how they have established the trade here, and with what clarity they have demonstrated the great losses sustained by the State, through the export of funds and the removal or emigration of the King's subjects. Nothing now will bring it back, nothing can reverse the flow of funds except the setting up of a great industry, with free manufacture and free export of raw materials, for the use of consumers in the Kingdom itself as well as abroad. In order to achieve this, the government must accord protection without distinction to all establishments throughout the Kingdom, but especially to those in Alsace granting free entry to the products of the said establishments'.

The Sierentz manufactory seems therefore to have been of only medium importance (40–60 tables) but unfortunately, we have at this time no samples whatever.

The fourth manufactory was that of 'Frères Dollfus, Vetter & Cie'. This was directed by Jean-Henri Dollfus and appears to have been set up in the first place to manufacture pure silk ribbons, from a process invented by George Zeller. It was compelled to establish itself on French territory at Dornach near Mulhouse. But due to hostility of the passementerie makers of Mulhouse, and despite official authorisation, the enterprise did not last long and heavy losses were incurred by the partners. In 1758, it undertook printing work as 'Koechlin, Dollfus and Cie' and from 1765–1786 as 'Jean-Henri Dollfus & Vetter', the two partners being Jean-Henri Dollfus and Jean Vetter, his brother-in-law. In 1786 it set up in the Cour de Lorraine under the name of 'Dollfus Père et Fils et Cie'. This establishment had the reputation of being in the first rank both through the perfection of its products and beauty of its designs. Thanks to the French Revolution, an excellent designer joined its ranks: Malaine Senior, a refugee at Mulhouse. The manufactory scored some great successes, but it did not last long. In 1794, Jean-Georges Dollfus left it to direct, at least for a time, the manufactory of wallpapers known as 'Nicolas Dollfus & Cie'. Nicolas Dollfus, the son of Jean-Jacques, left the wallpaper business to return to the new Company which now became 'Dollfus Père et Fils'. In 1797, Jean-Georges and Gaspard Weiss arrived on the scene. The name now became: "Dollfus Père, Fils, Weiss et Cie". It was engaged in copperplate printing importing big furniture designs from England. In 1800, it was directed by only one man: Nicolas Dollfus, and a sleeping partner holding 80,000 *livres* tournois until the year 1802, Jean-Henri Dollfus Senior, and a new name: 'Dollfus et Cie'.

This then was the story of our 'Three Musketeers', who were four, as is proper; the founders of the first manufactory at Mulhouse, politically a free Republic, but geographically sited in Upper Alsace.

After 'Koechlin, Schmaltzer et Cie', other manufactories of greater or lesser importance in terms of size, duration and quality emerged. A list of the main ones appears below, but we know very little about them in reality, as will be seen:

1752: 'Hartmann et Cie'; partners; Jean-Michel Hartmann, Jean Dollfus and Mathias Schmerber, dyer, (already mentioned page 11).

In 1775, this became 'Wolf, Risler et Cie', and in 1789, 'Wolf et Moser', and in 1796, 'Engel et Cie' with Jean-Henri Engel at its helm and a Christophe Burckhardt of Basle as a sleeping partner with 70,000 *livres* tournois.

In 1754, we find 'Anthes, Feer et Cie'.

In 1756, 'Hofer, Risler et Cie', which in 1780 became 'Risler, Dollfus et Cie', subsequently closing down in 1785.

From the partnership created in 1758 between J. J. Feer and Daniel and Henri Huguenin, there remained the manufactory named 'Frères Huguenin' in 1763. In 1773, it became, 'HUGUENIN l'Aîné', and continued in being as such until around the year 1840.

1760: 'Nicolas Risler et Cie' was directed by Nicolas Risler Père, J. Feer and Jérémie Hofer. In 1769, they were joined by Nicolas Risler Fils, Pierre Dollfus (1748–1830), Theodore Braun Junior (1740–1814) who later established himself at Villefranche (in the Beaujolais region some 30 kilometres from Lyon) in 1782.

In 1770, Pierre Dollfus takes over an establishment at Wesserling. The company then had two manufactories, one at Mulhouse and one at Wesserling. In 1772/3, the partners wanted to set up near Villefranche in the Beaujolais region a manufactory for making 'garas' (a crude type of heavy cloth) bringing in weavers and printers from Mulhouse, since these types of products were not made in the Beaujolais region. But they failed as the Mulhouse laws forbade to its citizens to create outside manufactures similar to those of the town.

The Mulhouse manufactory continued until 1793 when Pierre Dollfus and Nicolas Risler settled definitely at Thann.

About 1760 Abraham Schmaltzer set up a Manufactory, and his widow continued the business after his death, until the year 1790.

In 1760 or 1761 Jean Eck, Jean Hofer the tanner, Jean-Michel Schwartz and Jean-Jacques Kielmann set up a manufactory at Cour des Chaines (Kettenhof) in Mulhouse.

Between 1785 and 1790, the manufactory made a name for itself with its manufacture of puce-coloured shawls, well-produced and brilliantly designed by Jean-Ulric Nifenecker. In 1801, the name was changed to: 'Schwartz, Hofer et Cie' and set up at Cernay (Upper Alsace).

In 1764, Jean Dollfus (1729–1800), pharmacist and later Burgomaster, Jean Hofer (1746–1810) son-in-law of Jean Dollfus, Jean-Henri Dollfus, Jean's brother, set up the manufactory named 'Dollfus & Hofer', which later became 'Jean Dollfus' (Père et Fils) in 1777. In 1783 'Jean Dollfus Père' remained alone until 1790 at the 'Trois-Rois' at Mulhouse.

In 1790, we find the 'Heinrich & Cie' manufactory directed by Michel Heinrich. This became 'Pierre Risler & Cie' in 1795 and was directed by Pierre Risler Fils.

In 1764, J. J. Feer-Cornetz and Frederic Cornetz Junior, his brother-in-law, set up a printing works at Mulhouse under the name 'Feer et Cornetz'.

In 1778, Jean Hofer and Jérémie de Pierre Risler. The manufactory became 'Feer & Hofer'. On the death of J. J. Hofer in 1780 the name was changed to 'Jean Hofer & Cie'. Jean Hofer remained on his own in 1789. In 1790 Godefroi Heilmann and Jean de Fosué Hofer arrived and the name then became 'Heilmann, Hofer & Cie', with Jean Hofer Senior as the sleeping partner. In 1793, the enterprise was re-named yet again with the same name as it had during the first quarter of the 19th c.: 'Jean Hofer & Cie'. The partners were: Jean Hofer Senior, and Junior, and Pierre Schlumberger-Hartmann. This manufactory was the parent of several very large firms which sprang up during the 19th c. in both Mulhouse and its environs.

In 1765, 'Frank & Cie' became 'Huguenin, Reber & Cie' and in 1768, it disappeared at a time still unknown.

In 1764, we find: 'Heilmann, Blech & Cie'. This manufactory had an apprentice named Jean Zuber, who later on set up the famous wallpaper manufactory at Rixheim near Mulhouse. In 1793, the manufactory was renamed 'Blech, Schlumberger & Cie' and continued under various other names until the middle of the 19th c.

In 1764, we find: 'Thierry l'Aîné et Cie'. This was directed by Jean Dollfus from 1775 to 1777. It was still in existence in 1792 and possibly even longer than that date for the Pierre of Pierre Thierry, the mainspring of the enterprise, was still alive in 1799.

In 1767, 'Hartmann et Fils' became Tobie Hartmann Père et Fils in 1769 at the Rue Sainte-Claire. It went out of business in 1771.

In 1777, Paul of Paul Huguenin Fils, Jean Mantz Junior, Daniel Jelensperger and Nicolas Moser changed the cloth-mill of 'Jelensperger, Kohler & Cie' into 'Huguenin, Mantz & Cie'. with the object of adding a calico printing section. But in 1786, they changed the name again to 'Jelensperger, Thierry & Cie,' which name they retained until the business was liquidated in 1800–1803. One of the last of the partners therein, Heilmann-Frauger, went into the famous manufactory Dollfus–Mieg & Cie as managing director.

Around 1768 – 'Frederic Blech' was in business on his own; the enterprise later became 'Frederic Blech & Heilmann' in 1771, then 'Blech & Huguenin' in 1777, 'Vetter & Blech' in 1786, 'Vetter, Blech et Cie' in 1793, and 'Blech Fries & Cie, from 1796 to 1840.

This manufactory was the springboard for a very large and important firm which endured throughout the whole of the 19th c. renowned for its designers as much as for its chemists.

The *Ragionenbuch* (Register of Business enterprises) lists 42 manufactories, but gives no dates. According to our information, all of them were founded prior to 1769, but were of short duration. Since the list is very complex, we take the liberty of referring the reader to it himself, if he desires further details, and suggest that he may consult pages 427–430 of the Documentary History of the industry at Mulhouse. (See Bibliography).

Here, nevertheless are a few manufactories which were fairly short-lived:

In 1776, Kohler and Junghaen set up in the rue Paille at Mulhouse. This manufactory, which changed its name twice in the 18th c. ('Kohler, Junghaen & Meyer' in 1776 and 'Kohler & Junghaen' in 1795) was the origin of a very fine manufactory of the 19th c. and was greatly renowned.

In 1778, 'Schlumberger, Hartmann & Hirt' (became 'Schlumberger & Cie' in 1781) ceased trading in 1788.

1782: Martin Hartmann makes chintz alone, but joins with Jean-Gaspard Baumgartner in 1785. The manufactory changes its name to 'Baumgartner & Cie' in 1791, and ceases trading in 1821.

In 1786, 'Kielmann & Cie' appears, and continues until 1815 under the name of 'Risler, Koechlin & Cie'.

In 1786, we see 'Meyer, Schmaltzer & Cie': Painted fabrics.

Set up in 1788, 'Frères Blech & Cie' will continue in business until 1814 under the name 'Paul Blech & Cie'.

1791: Creation of 'Frères Thierry' (Pierre and Jean) which was dissolved in 1796.

1792: Daniel Schlumberger (1764–1827) works on his own at Mulhouse. The manufactory continued throughout all the 19th c. and became quite well-known.

1797: Jean-Jacques Danner, J. Georges Dollfus (1756–1825), Jean-Henri Stapfer, Rodolphe Grossmann and Jean Vetter Junior collaborate in the running of a manufactory of printed cloth at Dornach and a brewery at Lutterbach (both being close to Mulhouse) under the name of 'Dollfus, Vetter & Cie'. Towards the end of the year 1797, the partners split up: J. J. Danner leaves, and G. Dollfus and J. H. Stapfer take over the brewery, while J. Vetter and R. Grossmann carry on the manufacture under the name of: 'Grossmann & Cie'. In the month of Messidor Year VI (1798) Daniel of Jean Dollfus (1769–1818) came in as a sleeping partner, then later as an active partner in Germinal Year VIII (1800). The name became 'Dollfus-Mieg & Cie' on the 1st Germinal Year VIII (21 March 1800).

During the 19th c. the manufacture closed down its printing workshop and turned to the sewing thread side under the celebrated mark 'DMC' which became so well known.

Around 1798/99 a farmer named Jean Haeffely rented the old feudal stronghold of Pfastatt near Mulhouse; it was the property of the Zu-Rhein family. He tilled the soil and then launched later into a modest cloth bleaching, the material being supplied from the neighbouring villages after hand spinning and weaving. On his death in 1807, his son took over the business. He and his successors expanded it until it became of considerable importance during the 19th c. and 20th c. After one or two bad patches, the manufactory is today one of the leaders in its field in Europe, under the name: Société Nouvelle d'Impression de Pfastatt.

Mulhouse, though completely enclosed within the bounds of the French State until 1798 was the cradle and centre of textile printing in Upper Alsace and the manufactories which sprang up were to expand considerably during the course of the 18th century in the Vosges valleys:
Doller with Masevaux
Thur with Thann
Lauch with Guebwiller
Fecht with Munster.

We can find no printing work at Masevaux in the 18th century. Koechlin & Cie bought the possessions of the former chapter of Masevaux intending to found a textile printing works, but in reality established only cotton spinning, weaving and bleaching. Throughout the 19th and 20th century these industries kept the little town of Masevaux alive.

From Mulhouse as we proceed towards the Vosges, we come to Pfastatt and Lutterbach, both of which we mentioned earlier.

At Cernay 'Eck, Schwartz & Cie' of Mulhouse set up a manufactory here in 1801 under the name of 'Schwartz, Risler & Cie'.

In 1785–1786, Jean-Jacques Zurcher-Lischy of Mulhouse (1750–1839) founded the chintz manufactory of 'J. J. Zurcher & Cie' which produced printed scarves and handkerchiefs. J. J. Zurcher was for a long time employed in the calico printing works of Fasy at Geneva. It was said that one of the anecdotes which he enjoyed telling was of Voltaire's visit to the manufactory and since he did not want the old gentleman to have to use his stick Zurcher gave him his arm throughout the entire inspection. In 1796, J. J. Zurcher went into partnership with Henri Sandoz; in 1798 with Baudry; in 1816, J. Jacques Zurcher's son, replaced his father. The manufactory changed into a spinning mill and then left Cernay for Epinal (Vosges Department) where it remained during the whole of the 19th century to the beginning of the 20th century as a textile printing works. In 1800, it produced 6,000 pieces each of 16 Paris *aunes* (One *aune* equals 1.188 metres).

Another manufactory, that of 'Arnold Père et Fils' is listed in the year 1786, and was reported to possess 60 printing tables at that time.

Jean Witz founded a cloth printing works in 1791 under the name of 'Frères Witz & Cie'. This manufactory continued in business until 1839.

At Thann, we can find no trace of any manufactory prior to the years of the 19th century. But Wesserling, however, at the end of the valley, was quite another matter – indeed, it was a goldmine:–

On the 14th of May 1757 the deed of sale of the Château of Wesserling and its dependencies was signed by the Prince-Abbot and monks of the Abbey of Murbach and Lure, and one Desmarest, the King's tax gatherer for the Thann *départment*. The Chateau itself was built in 1635 by the Prince Abbé of Loewenstein, administrator of the Abbey of Murbach in the Saint-Amarin valley. It had been used as a hunting lodge. In 1762, Sandherr (of Colmar, Upper Alsace) and Desmarest requested authorization to found a manufactory for printed calicoes at Wesserling (Archives du Haut-Rhin at Colmar, document 1121–11).

On the 24th of March 1763, Desmarest was operating a fulling-mill, calender and bleaching works for the manufacture of printed cloth. He did not prosper and in 1773, he rented the property out to Sandherr and Courageot. These together fared no better and the property then went on lease to 'Nicolas Risler & Cie' manufacturers from Mulhouse. They set up a dyeing works, painting shop and in the surrounding villages they engaged hand-weavers and spinners.

In 1776, a fire ravaged the Château and part of the adjoining buildings. Nicolas Risler & Cie bought the entire estate for 15 or 16,000 *livres* tournois.

30 printing tables were installed, wood engraving was begun, a dyeing shop, and bleachery was set up. In two years some 150,000 *livres* flowed into a region that was hitherto poverty-stricken.

In 1780, the management was handed over to Pierre Dollfus of Mulhouse who rebuilt the Château in the form in which it still stands today.

In 1783 the manufactory now Pierre Dollfus & Cie, became a 'Manufacture Royale' under letters patent from the King, Louis XVI (this meant exemption from service in the militia for the workers, and exemption from the payment of certain taxes). There were 724 people employed: 20 engravers, 4 designers, 100 printers, 100 'tireurs' (children spreading the colouring matter in the sieve), 100 satiners, and 400 'pinceauteuses' (pencilling girls re-entering new colours by hand).

In 1787, Pierre Dollfus and Risler leaves Wesserling and the manufactory is renamed: 'Senn, Bidermann & Cie' of Geneva (Switzerland) who were associated with Risler & Cie since 1783.

In 1795, the manufactory is renamed 'Bourcart & Cie' until the year 1801, when Bourcart retires. The great assets of this particular manufactory, the only one with the title of 'Royale' of the whole region (no Mulhouse manufactory could of course be 'Royale'), spring from its technicians, naturally enough, but also from the genius of one designer: Dujardin. He was the first to undertake genre painting and this led on to personages but unlike the designs of J. B. Huet, the famous designer at the Oberkampf manufactory at Jouy-en-Josas near Versailles, Dujardin's work was not tinted in one but in several colours; copperplate for the black outline and woodblock work with relief engraving as the reproductions will show later on. The manufactory prospered throughout the 19th century and enjoyed an enviable reputation. Even today, under the control of the Comptoir de l'Industrie Cotonnière Boussac, it remains one of the most important in its field.

In the Lauch valley, calico printing came at a later date: In 1790, there was a cloth printing works at Guebwiller, that of 'J. J. Ziegler & Cie' but in 1805, this branched out into calico manufacture, bleachery, spinning and weaving sections. It was still functioning at the end of the 19th century.

The Fecht valley had two especially important manufactories: one at Logelbach, neighbourhood of Colmar, the other at Munster (not far from Colmar).

The Logelbach manufactory first appeared on the scene in 1775, as a result of the collaboration between the Haussman brothers, sons of a Colmar apothecary. One of them was Jean-Michel, of Logelbach (Colmar 1749 – Strasbourg 1825) an eminent chemist, who corresponded with Vauquelin, Berthollet and Gay-Lussac.

The principal discoveries which emerged from his workshop were:

1. A high degree of perfection in discharging (enlevage) aluminium and iron mordants; he used oxalic and tartaric acids.

2. Use of tin salts for so-called applied colours (i.e., not dyed).

3. Coloured dischargings.

4. Application of Prussian blue in one operation by means of iron oxide and prussiate of potash.

5. Use of acetate and indigo sulphates for pistachio green and Saxe green.

6. Nitrate of iron for application of black (i.e., not dyed).

7. Calcium as one of the elements necessary for the composition and strength of red madder dye. He added chalk to madder dyes in 1776. This move was made necessary by the difference in the type of water in Normandy where he worked first and in Logelbach. The latter did not allow him to obtain the same kinds of reds as the ones used in Normandy unless chalk were added.

In point of fact, the Abbé Mazéas, Canon of the Cathedral at Vannes, in his work entitled: 'Method to be used in France for production of red colouring on cotton fabrics, based on the process used in India', which was probably written prior to the year 1757, made a mordant based on alum, red dye-wood and lime. (The red dye-wood was used to lend some colour to the otherwise colourless alum). One wonders if Haussmann had ever heard of this work. We cannot be sure.

Jean, called Jean of Augsburg (Colmar 1740 –Wintzenheim near Colmar 1820) a businessman. Earlier, he began in the Schüle works at Augsburg, the Oberkampf of Germany, in 1770 he married the only daughter of Johann-Heinrich Edler von Schülé. On the death of his wife in 1772, he left for Rouen to found a manufactory of printed cloth in the 'faubourg Saint-Hilaire by the Robecque Canal' with, it would appear, one or two of his brothers. He made use of the mordant formulae used by the Schüle works, and he had then 12–15 printing tables. But he soon saw that the high cost of labour at Rouen was an obstacle to further expansion and he left Rouen for Logelbach. He also set up, in the meantime, a warehouse and shop near the Court at Versailles.

Christian Haussmann, known as the Doctor (Colmar 1738 – Paris 1800). After his marriage to a wealthy heiress of Colmar, he became the sleeping partner, and by seniority the head and master of Logelbach.

Marie-Madeleine (Colmar 1763 – Versailles 1806) married in 1782 Louis André Jordan, from Berlin, a descendant of Calvinist refugees from the south of France who fled as a result of the Edict of Nantes in 1685.

In 1776, the manufactory became the 'King's privileged Manufactory'.

And on the 3rd of October 1777, it became: 'Haussmann, Emmerich, Jordan & Cie'.

In this new manufactory we find Emmerich of Augsburg and Henri Riegé, a printer, also from Augsburg, and formerly employed as an inspector in the printing section of the Fridau manufactory (Austria). He left there after a dispute. On the 20th of October 1778, after a legal dispute once more, he left Logelbach and went to the Schmaltzer manufactory at Munster (not far from Logelbach).

In 1777, the Logelbach manufactory employed 400 workers. By the end of the Ancien Régime, it had between 1200 and 1500 workers, including women for pencilling and children employed in the washing and exposure of the goods upon meadows.

In the early days, the supplies of white fabric came from Switzerland; in 1786 weaving was begun in the villages of the Vosges region, but the Swabian and Franconian printers were still encouraged to come to the manufactory. In 1785, production reached 50,000 pieces valued at 2,400,000 *livres*. 75% of the production was exported to either the Leipzig and Frankfort Fairs, or to other markets such as Augsburg (a circular dated 1779 announced the manufacture of luxury articles with gold and silver thread in the selvedge in competition with the Bavarian manufactory i.e., Schüle) the Baltic countries, Russia, and France (Alsace was considered from the point of view of Customs as a foreign province till the revolution of 1789). The fabrics passed through the tax office at Saint-Dizier and from there went to the Versailles warehouse. Madame de Pompadour had made chintz very much the fashion; printed cottons were worn everywhere, even in the remotest villages around Versailles. At the beginning of the century the young girls of all the villages of Alsace referred to their dresses as their 'Pompatturs'.

The most ordinary types of printed goods were sent to the Antilles for barter trade through the port of Nantes.

The Logelbach manufactory also sent its goods to the Bordeaux Fair where they had a chequered history, Even though the Alsatians were 'foreigners in matters of trade, they were also subjects of the King' and they were able to keep their privileged status as foreigners regarding customs regulations.

The French Revolution however dealt a severe blow to the manufactory: from a total of 1,000 workers in 1792, there remained only 400 in 1797! The Versailles shop closed down in 1795: its administrator went on the local constitutional council of 1790.

Paper money also had a disastrous effect on the firm which more or less disintegrated in 1800/1806. But the bad patch was only temporary: under the name of 'Haussmann Frères' it flourished anew during the 19th century and still exists as a velvet weaving plant well known today.

We saw earlier that Jean-Jacques Schmaltzer Senior, one of the four pioneers of textile printing at Mulhouse went to Munster in 1776, some 20 kilometres west of Colmar. According to the Haussmann brothers, it was a 'very restricted establishment' having 12 to 15 tables and its prices (certainly low for that period) 'from 40 to 50 *sols* per aune'.

In 1778, Henri Riegé arrived from Logelbach. He bought Schmaltzer's tables and named the firm: 'Henri Riegé & Cie'. He had no right, though, to set up within six leagues of Colmar. He set up a sleeping partnership with Pourtalès & Cie at Neuchâtel. The minutes of the suit brought by the Haussmann brothers against H. Riegé tell us that 'Mr. Pourtalès and his firm cede all the tools and sell 17 fully equipped tables at Munster'. In the same report we learn that in 1784 the manufactory possessed 'three times more tables than heretofore (prior to 1779) (which means from 36 to 45 tables) and 'that it was working finer qualities'. In 1785, the Manufactories Inspector notes that Henri Riegé & Cie is still being supplied by Pourtalès in calicoes.

In 1790, after a dispute, Henri Riegé left the manufactory. This man seems to have had a decidedly difficult personality! The manufactory then became: 'André Hartmann and Sons', Frédéric, Jacques and Henri, It still retains the sleeping partnership share of Pourtalès & Cie. In 1799, the firm joined with Soehnée l'Aîné & Cie of Paris. It was not until 1818 that the firm adopted its final name which carried it over into the 20th century to its great renown: 'Hartmann et Fils' –

As regards Ribeauvillé, situated on the Strengbach, a tributary of the Fecht, we know from the Rupied Manuscript: 'The art of cloth printing in Alsace' (1786) (see Bibliography) that this charming little town employed 1,200 people both for the running of the manufactory and the working of the cloth which it wove and printed itself. It produced 6,000 pieces of from 15 to 16 *aunes*, which at the average price of 40 *livres* each gave the province a net profit of 240,000 *livres*.

The last of the Vosges valleys which undertook textile printing in Upper Alsace was that of Liepvrette with Sainte-Marie-aux-Mines as the main centre.

The main business of Sainte-Marie was weaving and dyeing of wool cloth, but the famous questionnaire filled in in 1772 by Mr. d'Aigrefeuille, Manufactories Inspector for Alsace, for the Abbé Terray, who was responsible for the Royal Treasury at Versailles, provides us with some precious items of information:–

'The valley of Sainte-Marie, population some five thousand souls, has been galvanised into activity on a scale hitherto unknown. In 1756, under the name of Fabrique Ducale des Deux-Ponts, a manufactory of chintz, dimity, siamese, fustian and *toile de Paris*, was set up on unused land belonging to M. le Duc de Deux-Ponts'.

But this is the history of a manufactory of German origin and lies outside the scope of our work here.

What types of printing was carried on in Mulhouse and in Upper Alsace during this period? The answers to the question can be found from an examination of two main sources: The Rupied Manuscript dated 1786, which has so far never been published. Rupied was a 'Manufactories apprentice', attached to the Manufactories Inspectorate for the province of Alsace, based at Colmar. Inspector Buob charged Rupied with the task.

The second source is the range of samples held by the *Musée de l'Impression sur Etoffes de Mulhouse*.

Let us first of all see what Rupied has to say: 'There are several kinds – *calanca, demi-calanca,* ordinary chintz, *patenace*, camaieu, double blue, double violet, camaieu in all colours, mourning chintz, handkerchiefs which are reversible, etc. The designer has to be able to work in all these kinds, observing simplicity in design, avoiding any running or confusion of colours, and holding to one dominant theme, either in the matter of flowers or the tints which his brush lends to his design.

Calancas are almost always in floral design. Black is used for delineation and there can be up to three reds. The quality of the cloth used in this type of manufacture must go hand in hand with the beauty of design, varied to an infinite degree. Only one or two colours are used in common chintz, black or red or black and red. The colours used may be brought out still more by picot work, or by perpendicular, horizontal or diagonal hatching.

Patenaces are merely ordinary chintz but of better quality than those mentioned above. Blue and yellow are added and applied one on the other and produce greens.

The best cloth must be used for special work (*petites façons*) for this type of printing can produce some very beautiful effects. The flowers must be very small and spaced out with care and the exercise of taste; small picot work is also used for this type of production. Double blue work is engraved in black and the flowers all shaded so that in using violet for the half-tints with a general blue ground, the result is a blue camaieu; triple blue is done by application of one violet under and two blues over.

Red camaieu work and double violet work is carried out in the same manner; the only difference as regards the latter is that it is printed in a red-brown which is referred to as fine red.

Mourning calicoes require black ground and white flowers, as well as white flowers with black flowers; shagreening and picot work are also used. Reversible handkerchiefs are produced by application of the blocks to each side and so adroitly that it seems as if both sides were painted with one stroke.

All these types are made in Alsace, especially handkerchiefs No. 4 and No. 5 for children. Some very pretty furniture chintz are executed on all types of cloth; one Mulhouse firm sends to Leghorn and Genoa large "carpets" with which the Italian women cover themselves from head to foot. These articles are printed on a white ground on guinea or swabian cloth. They measure $2\frac{1}{2}$ *aunes* by $1\frac{3}{4}$ *aunes*.

In conclusion, I would say that if a fine, close and well-executed weave ensures a ready sale for printed cloth, it is no less important that its variety and elegant design meet the consumer's requirements; the Alsatian products have all these advantages plus freshness and strength of colour. The Manufactories of Colmar and Wesserling are known mainly for their brilliant colours, and the intense whiteness of the fabric used. The limpid water at their disposal undoubtedly gives them an advantage over competitors.'

All manufacturers had their own designers and were able, furthermore, to call on Parisian artists for certain sketches. The famous Pillement, painter to the King of Poland and Queen Marie Antoinette, was responsible for a number of Chinese designs, and real or imagined flowers in line with the Chinese fashion of the 18th century. Gergogne, painter to King Stanislas (1677–1766) at Nancy supplied André Hartmann at Munster and Haussmann at Logelbach with designs in the oriental style.

Figure number 9 in the reproductions is signed by 'Gergogne'.

Since the flower was the basic element in almost all designs, it was to the painter of flowers that the textile printers turned. And later, they specialised in design for textile printing, as was the case with Malaine Senior (1745–1809), painter of flowers for King Louis XVIth at the Gobelins Manufactory (1787). He also worked for the Sèvres manufactory and the wallpaper manufactory of Folie-Titon. He was arrested at Belfort in 1793 because he was adjudged to be a member of the King's Household. He was saved by the people of Mulhouse who sheltered him during the reign of Terror. He joined the manufactory of Dollfus Senior and Sons and then went to the wallpaper manufactory of Hartmann Risler, predecessors of the Zubers at Rixheim near Mulhouse. He executed some remarkable designs for them. He returned to Paris after the Revolution. He died in 1809 on the very day of his nomination as professor to the Lyon Academy. His son, Louis-Joseph-Alphonse, (1782–1858) born in Paris, the devoted student of his father's techniques, started his working life at the Gobelins. Then he went to the Thann manufactory as a designer and later, (1810) to Koechlin brothers' manufactory at Mulhouse, where he stayed 42 years. He specialised in cashmere designs for which he was celebrated.

Jean-Georges Hirn (1777–1839) was a native of Mulhouse. He took lessons in design from the brother of the famous astronomer Lambert, then went to Constance (Germany) for several years. Jean-Michel Haussmann became interested in his talents and sent him to Paris to study flower painting. His training over, he returned to Logelbach where he married Jean-Michel Haussmann's daughter and became a partner in the firm of 'Haussmann, Jordan, Hirn & Cie'. He was best known for his designs of flower backgrounds in the Pompadour style and specialised in medallions for silk scarves. But he became famous in the 19th century especially.

Marie-Bonaventure Lebert Senior (1759–1836) arrived in Alsace from Paris in 1786 and joined Pierre Dollfus. 'An artist of great talent and an honest man', he was born in Paris. His father (1722–1782) a master designer and a logically-minded man sent his son to study at the academy run by J. M. Vien, the teacher of David. Later, he became a student under Delaunay and Née. Pierre Dollfus sent for him in 1782, as also for his younger brother, Jean-Baptiste Lebert (1788–1873), who was then still studying. He worked for Mulhouse, Wesserling and Logelbach. For the most part, he lived at Thann and here he met many artist friends: Saint-Quentin, the King's painter, Malaine, Tardieu, Duval and Henri Hofer. M.B. Lebert had a collection of plaster casts of well-known works sent to him from Paris, which he copied in the evenings. For the manufactory, he designed panels seven feet high in tapestry fashion in which figures from the style of Watteau or Boucher stood out against a background of landscape, parkland or architectural features. For furniture decoration he imitated older cameos; on waistcoats styles which were then in fashion he designed subjects from Lafontaine and La Nouvelle Heloise. Figure number 80 is certainly his work. In 1788 he returned to Paris and lived through the exaltation of the revolutionary era. At first enthusiastic, the death of Louis XVI horrified him. He returned to Thann in 1790, but not before he had carried out a number of etchings, especially portraits of Franklin. The great panel of the Musée de l'Impression, which was executed at Wesserling in Year XII and printed by Jean Koechlin, is dedicated to Benjamin Franklin. This is probably one of his works, as well as the other two of the same type (Figure number 37).

While Jean-Baptiste Lebert remained at Wesserling his elder brother accepted in 1796 the offer of an appointment with the firm of Hartmann's at Munster.

Among other well-known designers of the 18th century we must mention: Portalier, Linguet, Prévot, St. Quentin, Villeneuve, Birr and Rodolphe Koechlin.

Jean-François Grosjean, born in 1774 at Sélestadt (Lower Alsace), a pupil of David, also leaves a remarkable name among the famous printing designers, but this was not to be until 1803 when he returned to Alsace.

Emmanuel Fries (1778–1850), born in Mulhouse, underwent his artistic apprenticeship at Paris with Regnault from 1794–1797, then returning to Blech-Fries to work there from 1797–1823.

But how many others must there be under the cloak of anonymity, excellent designers all of them, the heroes of the profession.

All these designs are inspired by the original chintz from which they are derived. There are simple and straightforward designs, charming in their simplicity and their candour, as in figure numbers 67, 110, 111, 119, 120, 121 and 123. (These last four have just been redrawn for the current market). Normally, they have only two colours: red and black. Sometimes there is a little yellow, or pink or violet. From what we have read in the Rupied manuscript we might be led to thinking that these are for common chintz and the *patenas* for these. Among the decorative elements, there is the medallion of either oval or very simple round shape, with its vermiculations and picot work, all just to bring out or enhance the simplest of humble flowers.

Other designs resemble the Pompadour style, such as those in figure numbers 24 and 35, delightfully beribboned tulips. More whimsical still, but still in the same style are the little flowers in picot or the poppies alternating with peacocks and other strange birds in figure number 102.

But entirely with the Pompadour spirit even though the same theme is not present we find the little designs of baskets of fruit and ears of wheat in figure number 70. These are very probably the 'petites façons' mentioned by Rupied.

Flowered stripes are characteristic of Louis XVIth, but this particular one while elegant and fine drawn is not the best; it is simple and charming with its garland of crucifers, edging of small apples and flowers just a little bit on the exotic side. (Figure numbers 8, 43, 83, 116 and 118). Rather more severe and somewhat curious is that in figure number 88 with a type of column design; it looks as though it could have been designed by an architect. But is this not rather the severity of the Directory period that is being heralded here?

Figure number 7 is remarkable for its arabesques. Perhaps this is rather to misuse the word when we are dealing only with simple undulating branches, bent back in support here and there, and a small flower or a small round leaf. (See also figure number 15). Might these not be *calancas*? The latter theme is really only an Indian inspiration which has been completely transformed by local thinking. There are many designs of oriental conception, sometimes influenced to a greater or lesser degree by the Pillement style. (See figure number 106) where garlands very much in the style of Louis XVIth hang in the flowered branches of trees which are very European in style. And from the garlands, here and there, appears a flower in the form of a pagoda! The same thing applies to figure number 52 where, lost amidst the flowers and surmounting a rococo Louis XV impression, we see four little Chinese bells whose topmost points are decorated with three sets of four points. These famous four points which are so often encountered in Indian designs are possibly symbolic, but we have no information on this subject.

In a more pure form of Pillement styling, the Musée de l'Impressions sur Etoffes possesses a magnificent design, see figure number 26 where a kind of reversed cone, suspended to a bush, is joined to it by a Louis XVI knot.

Figure number 81 presents, as with certain designs from India and taken up by Jouy pineapples mixed with ranunculus and irises. Figure number 95 is also very curious; it is by Lehmann, and is directly inspired by oriental plants.

But of particular interest is figure number 47 which is shown as being from the Haussmann manufactory at Logelbach, dated 1777/1778, and thus one of the first made there. This design is the very image of a pezzoto. The pezzoto is a small veil from Genoa, whose proper name is a Mezzaro, with the form and measurements of a large scarf (about 1.10 mètres × 2.30 mètres). We know that the motifs which appear on the mezzaro are directly inspired by those found on Indian palempora: the tree of life on its mount with an extraordinary decor of flowers, butterflies, birds and animals of all descriptions. Here again, we have a whole line of trees of life, each on its own mount. We know that one of the first manufacturers of mezzari at Genoa was Speich, originally from Glaris (Switzerland). Rupied says that Alsace was supposed to have executed veils for Genoa in the 18th century. Might not this be proof of this fact?

Of a rather different kind, a sort of compromise between the calanca and the fabric with designs of personages, are these Chinese polychromes, figure number 57, which are very amusing: a small Chinaman seated on a flower, at the foot of a small bush, holding two hearts captive, so preventing them from flying away. All this is set in a scene which is in scale with the personages represented. This type of design is familiar at this period of time, or slightly earlier at Jouy, the 'little fisherman' and the 'little hunter'.

We also find designs of oriental inspiration on a black ground known as 'Ramoneur', a ground which could also be brown or dark red. See figure number 9, signed Godinot and Gergogne. We know almost nothing about Godinot, except that he worked for Nicolas Risler at Mulhouse. (Figure numbers 44 and 93).

Some of these designs mix fruit and flowers, tropical and European plants, all together, see figure numbers 46, 60 and 63, and in the latter there are poppies, maize, and daisies. Our delightful little mountain flowers, so pure and fresh, also inspired our designers: figure number 113, where on a 'Ramoneur' ground we find wild strawberries, campanulas, lily of the valley, forget-me-nots, plantains and white campion.

And at the very end of the century we find the style known as 'bonnes herbes' on white ground, figure number 36 or on a 'ramoneur' ground figure number 92 – a style which was enthusiastically taken up by Parisian stylists in 1964 when they rediscovered them once more.

A little out of the mainstream of classic Indian prints are the camaïeux. These are machine-printed, a sort of press with flat blocks: copperplate of some 90 centimètres wide. Only one panel could be printed at any one time and therefore only one colour, hence the name. All the various tints and hues are obtained by special engraving, and for this reason, the design is very light and detailed. These are shown in figure numbers 11 and 55. These two charming designs in red are filled with tiny allegories of Love: fiery torches, shepherd's crooks, Marie-Antoinette hats, entwined hearts above a bow and arrow, thatched cottages in medallions held by two knotted ribbons. Figure number 13 is printed in blue *faïencé*. The flower design, also a charming display, is however a little less light in tone. This magnificent work is attributed to Huguenin the Elder and is one of the rare examples of this type of blue *faïencé*, a colour certainly much less common than the red camaïeu. The surrounding design is enriched by several threads of gold forming squares and these add to the beauty of both the design and the engraving work.

All these examples of flowered polychrome or camaïeux designs whether wood block or copper-plate were also used for printing designs on clothing: waistcoats, dresses, etc., and for furnishing fabrics: curtains, bedcovers, armchair coverings, etc... and especially for wall coverings and in alcoves in an age when wallpapers were almost unknown. In the period 1750–1770, even until 1780, the same design was used for both dress or furnishing. But this was not the case from 1780 onwards where the prints carry figures whose subject is primarily one for use in furnishings. These were for the most part Dujardin's designs, which he executed for the Wesserling manufactory: 'La Litière', 'Le Repos familial', 'La Halte', and 'L'Escarpolette', which were used in printing, as will be seen from the two examples at the Musée de l'Impression sur Etoffes: 'La Charrette du Dimanche'. The designer also sometimes composed the motif from the type of seat he was to cover: such as the charming design of the harvester in medallion, surrounded by corn stalks and cornflowers, or the antique pitcher encircled by vine-branches. These were very probably composed by Dujardin under Louis XVI, as may be seen by reference to figure number 29 entitled: 'Le Faune et l'Enfant' and which still possesses the insignia of the Royal Manufactory.

If furnishing fabric designs had its own specialities, dress was certainly not forgotten. This admirable man's waistcoat very probably designed by M. B. Lebert for Munster at the very end of the 18th century bears witness to this. The waistcoat is ready for cutting out by the tailor – neither the buttons, nor the lapels, nor the trimmings are missing. (Figure number 80).

For putting away their little store of embroidered cambric handkerchiefs, ladies could buy handkerchief cases, which also did duty as work cases; they were delightful little squares printed with designs of flowers in Indian style (figure number 23) or with some appropriate motif thereon, as exemplified by the splendid figure number 18 dated about 1790, which represents on the front a richly decorated composition of the purest Louis XVIth style and on the back a seascape of very sober type. This type of scene is very odd when one considers that the nearest ports to Mulhouse are Genoa or Amsterdam! Perhaps we should read into this a trace of the great influence of trade by sea with the Far East which affected our city, and contributed to its economic expansion.

But now we must look at the handkerchiefs, those small and insignificant scraps of cloth which were so useful, serving for all sorts of ends. It has to undergo every kind of test. Creative imagination would be allowed free rein.

The first handkerchiefs were very simple and unassuming: small squares, stripes along the edges, and of one colour: figure numbers 5 and 6 from Feer and Huguenin in 1760.

Soon they would be used to illustrate great moments in history along the lines of the Epinal example. An occurrence like the 'Ascension de la Montgolfière' set many minds at work (figure number 12). Everybody took pleasure in carrying this little gem about in his or her pocket or bag. Sometimes, they depict ordinary events ... What exactly happened when this red camaïeu handkerchief was printed by Heinrich Koechlin in 1785? (figure number 13). On a very amusing little square, surrounded by a satirical commentary on the high headgear and wigs of the women of that era, it would seem that the central motif has been reprinted. A motif whose significance still escapes us is repeated four times: two lions with intertwined tails in the form of a bretzel (an Alsatian cake) hold shovels and tanners scrapers. Below, three clusters of grapes. In the centre, a medallion with the arms of the city of Mulhouse (the mill wheel – the word Mulhouse comes from Mühle – Mülhausen in German) and the name of Heinrich Koechlin. Who was he? It seems that this must be Jean-Henri Koechlin-Huguenin (1758–1835) son of Samuel Koechlin the founder of the Mulhouse industry and of Elizabeth Hofer. In 1780, he was admitted without entry fee to the Guild of Tailors, the same which included the calico printers of Mulhouse. In that same year, he married Rosine Huguenin, daughter of Daniel Huguenin the Elder, a manufacturer of chintz. When he was in the process of buying a house, we find him described as a 'manufacturer'. The Koechlin's family tree describes him as the almoner of a hospital, and the Documentary History of the Industry at Mulhouse mentions him as 'a partner of his father-in-law, Daniel Huguenin the Elder' until 1792. Is this handkerchief a souvenir of his family, or a gift from his friends at the time of his marriage or perhaps at the moment when he was admitted to the Guild of Tailors? Or is it perhaps a trial item made by himself? We do not know.

A third handkerchief, also very amusing, represents the so popular Frederick II, King of Prussia. Even though he is not named, the artist has written in the pithy sentence: 'It is to see and admire you that I keep you in my handkerchief'. This design is probably copied from an engraving by Johan Esaïas Nilson, engraver at Augsburg (Germany). (1721–1788) and the handkerchief itself could date from about 1763 (Peace of Hubertsburg). The King of Prussia was very popular in Alsace throughout the 18th century. He is seen here at the beginning of his reign in the uniform of Colonel of his Regiment of Foot Guards. The fortress in the background is probably that of the city of Breslau, taken in 1740 during the first Silesian War.

But the term handkerchief can also be applied to much larger squares: headscarves. The same motif can be applied as to the smaller surfaces. No one is in any doubt about the quality of Alsatian table-cloths, and these are but larger sizes still of the same thing. Their reputation is still as good today as it was in the past. All of these handkerchiefs or small cloths have the same characteristics: one-colour ground (figures number 21 and 38) more or less covered with a carpet of flowers, figures number 99 and 104, or and which is rarer, a uniform design (figure number 68). All their beauty and wealth of expression is to be found in the edging. These are sometimes of extraordinary elegance and refinement, like the ferns in camaïeu of figure number 21, allied to a pure and simple style which is evident at the end of the Louis XVI era. Even when they are simpler in design, they are nevertheless filled with charm and delight (figure number 109). Others on the contrary are positively opulent, richly filled, but though a little heavy, by no means altogether tasteless, as is this half-handkerchief, printed by the Haussmann brothers at Logelbach.

The edgings are really so beautiful that many of our manufacturers have set about printing them purely for themselves and they have become in our modern world a much admired trimming: they appear on dresses, table-cloths, curtains, even on walls.

Notes

1. Partial colouring of cotton in the 'Indian' fashion, where the colours stay fast (that is, where they resist air, light, and repeated washing) is obtained after a complicated process. Mordants (metallic salts) such as aluminium sulphate (alum) and iron acetate are used. These do not dye in themselves but combine, according to their degree of concentration and mixture one with another, to provide a range of colours such as reds, pinks, violets, browns and blacks, with Chayaver alizarin, Indian madder. The colour is then fixed on the cotton cloth insolubly. But prior to all this, the material has to be prepared by means of a stringent (tannin) culled from plants, and by means also of buffalo milk, a fatty substance. Blues are applied directly by immersion in a vat of indigo, those parts which it is desired should remain white being protected by a layer of wax. This was also used when the dyers wanted to obtain particularly fine white or red lines. The design was traced out in the wax and treated with the mordant which only affected the unprotected parts, leaving the rest white. The only colour which was effective was yellow, this being obtained from certain plants. Mixed with some alum and overlaid on blue it provided green, but since this did not stand up to a washing, it faded within a fairly short time. This explains why calicoes from older times rarely have green colouring in them. 'Painted' cloth was in reality then 'dyed' cloth, from whence they derived their resistance and hence their success. Mordants were laid on the cloth either by means of a special brush, or a wooden block with raised engraving (in this case in a thickened state).

2. The citizens of Mulhouse were divided into six 'Tribes': Vintners, Tailors, Butchers, Bakers, Farmers, Blacksmiths. They grouped many corporations, very different one from the other. Amongst the 'Tailors' for instance, you could find in 1790, 23 corporations; merchants, dyers, chemists, wig makers, bookbinders, etc. The first chintz-printer appears on June 23rd 1756, and the first engraver on December 20th 1765.

3. The importance of a manufactory is measured in numbers of printing tables. It would have been interesting to follow the developments of the Mulhouse calico printers through their accounts, but unfortunately there are no records of this type for the whole period of the 18th century. The municipal archives do have fiscal documents, but only for certain years, and this gives us some information on the size of some manufactories.
For the year 1783, for example, we see that Huguenin, Mantz & Cie paid 615 *livres*, the lowest amount on the list, whereas the highest tax was 3,765 *livres* paid by J. H. Dollfus & Vetter, the second on the list being Nicolas Risler & Cie with 3,566 *livres*. These two enterprises alone during the year 1783 paid more than a quarter of the taxes levied on the manufacturers of printed fabrics. That was at the rate of 5/12%, we can thus arrive at the turnover figure of the manufactories taxed, which was around 900,000 *livres* for the one which contributed the most, in the year 1783, and less than 150,000 *livres* for the one which contributed the least. During that same year, 21 manufactories were taxed; 27 in 1786, with Dollfus Père Fils et Cie in the lead with 4,545 *livres*, and the second reaching only 2,127 *livres*, the firm being Heilmann, Dollfus & Cie.
We know nothing about how sales were organised, whether of expensive or cheap goods, but taking prices of 50 *livres* and 25 *livres* per piece of 15/16 *aune* (Paris measurements) in ¾ widths (one aune equals 1.188 metres), a turnover figure of one million *livres* would give 20,000 pieces of top quality or 40,000 pieces at 25 *livres* of ordinary quality.

4. Porcelaine is a resist-blue as we said before, Finschitz=Feinschitz, Cubschitz=Küpenschitz, words which mean Fine-Chintz and vat-chintz, a quality where the blue came from the indigo-vat, the places already dyed in different colours being protected by a resist paste. Peruvians have still a vague signification as printed goods.

5. Patenar=Patnas, Suratter=Surate, Pulvinater (yet undetermined). Toiles d'Orange means perhaps an imitation of the production of that town.

6. This Swiss competition was mainly the Mulhouse one, its inhabitants being considered at that time as Swiss.

Bibliography

Publications of the Société Industrielle de Mulhouse (founded 1826, declared of public utility 1832).

Histoire documentaire de l'industrie à Mulhouse (Documentary history of the industry at Mulhouse, Mulhouse, 1902.

Quarterly Bulletins:

III/IV 1946, Bi-centenaire de l'impression en Alsace (Bi-centenary of textile printing in Alsace, 1746–1946).

III/1950, I/1951, I/1952, P. R. SCHWARTZ, Les débuts de l'indiennage mulhousien (Beginning of the Mulhouse printing industry, first creation by Mulhouse of a factory in Upper Alsace, new research work in unpublished documents of the Mulhouse municipal archives).

I/1966 P. R. SCHWARTZ, La fabrique d'indiennes du Duc de Bourbon (1692–1740) au Château de Chantilly (The chintz manufacture of the Duke of Bourbon at his Chantilly Castle). First publication of 2 anonymous treatises concerning printing before 1740.

IV/1962 P. R. SCHWARTZ, Les toiles peintes indiennes (Indian chintz).

I/1967 P. R. SCHWARTZ, L'impression sur coton à Ahmedabad (Indes) en 1676 (Cotton printing in Ahmedabad in 1678, first publication of the ROQUES manuscript, Bibliothèque Nationale in Paris).

Studies in Indo-European Textile History, by John IRWIN and P. R. SCHWARTZ, Calico Museum of Textiles, Ahmedabad, 1966 (up to date republication of studies published in the Journal of Indian Textile History, contains the first English translation of the BEAULIEU ms, concerning cotton painting at Pondicherry in 1734, and the first complete and exact translation of Father COEURDOUX's letter of 1742 regarding the same matter and town.

A century of French fabrics, 1850–1950, F. LEWIS, Leigh-on-Sea, 1964, P. R. SCHWARTZ & R. de MICHEAUX.

La toile imprimée et les indiennes de traite, Henry-René d'ALLEMAGNE, GRÜND, Paris 1942 (Printed cloth and chintz for African trade).

Etat des Manufactures de toiles et de Draps de Haute-Alsace de 1756 à 1772, L. RICHARD 1967 (List of cloth manufactures in Upper-Alsace, 1756–1772, from study of files in the National Archives, Paris,– unpublished, kept in the archives of the Mulhouse Société d'Histoire et Sciences naturelles).

Catalogue of the exhibition of printing at Wesserling, XVIII & XIXth centuries, organized by the Musée de l'Impression sur Etoffes de Mulhouse in 1967.

L'art d'imprimer sur toile en Alsace, RUPIED, 1786 (Cotton printing in Alsace, 1786, ms. never published, kept in the National Archives, Paris, photocopy Library of the Musée de l'Impression sur Etoffes de Mulhouse).

Notes sur les HAUSSMANN et la Manufacture du Logelbach, jusqu' en 1830, Paul LEUILLIOT, Annuaire de la Société Historique et Littéraire de Colmar 1951–1952 (Notes concerning the HAUSSMANN and the Logelbach manufactory, Yearbook 1951–1952 of the Colmar Historical & Literary Society).

Généalogie de la famille HAUSSMANN, Philippe MIEG (Genealogy of the HAUSSMANN family, 1964 Yearbook of the above Colmar society). The famous Baron Haussmann (1809-1891), creator of modern Paris, belongs to this family.

Archives of the HAUSSMANN enterprise, still existing as a weaving plant. Law suit against a former partner, Jean-Henri RIEGE, manufacturer at Munster, 1784).

Marie-Bonaventure LEBERT, artiste parisien (1759–1836) et sa contribution à l'art du dessin à Thann. Annuaire de la Société d'Histoire des régions de Thann-Guebwiller, 1961–1964 (Contribution of a Parisian artist M. B. LEBERT to the art of design at Thann, Yearbook of the Historical Society of the regions Thann-Guebwiller).

La toile peinte en France au XVIIe et au XVIIIe siècles, Edgard DEPITRE, Paris 1912 (History of the prohibition laws against the fabrication of chintz in France from 1686 to 1759).

Livre d'or de la Ville de Mulhouse, Nicolas EHRSAM, révisé par Louis SCHOENHAUPT, Mulhouse 1883 (Golden book of the city of Mulhouse, till its union in 1798 with the French Republic, historical part and family names).

Lettre du 13 août 1965 de Monsieur P. MARTIN, conservateur du Musée Historique de Strasbourg concernant le mouchoir représentant Frédéric II de Prusse, possédé par le Musée de l'Impression sur Etoffes de Mulhouse (Letter of the keeper of the Strasbourg Historical Museum, concerning the handkerchief representing Frederick II of Prussia, in possession of the Musée).

Fig. 1   Chintz. Mulhouse. c. 1780

Fig. 2   Corner of table-cloth. By Heilmann, Dollfus & Cie., or Heilmann, Père et Fils.
Mulhouse. 1790–1805

Fig. 3   Handkerchief. "Frederick II King of Prussia". After the
engraving by Johann Esaias Nilson of Augsburg (1721–1788).
Alsace, possibly Logelbach. c. 1750

Fig. 4   Handkerchief. By Huguenin the Elder. Mulhouse 1785

5

6

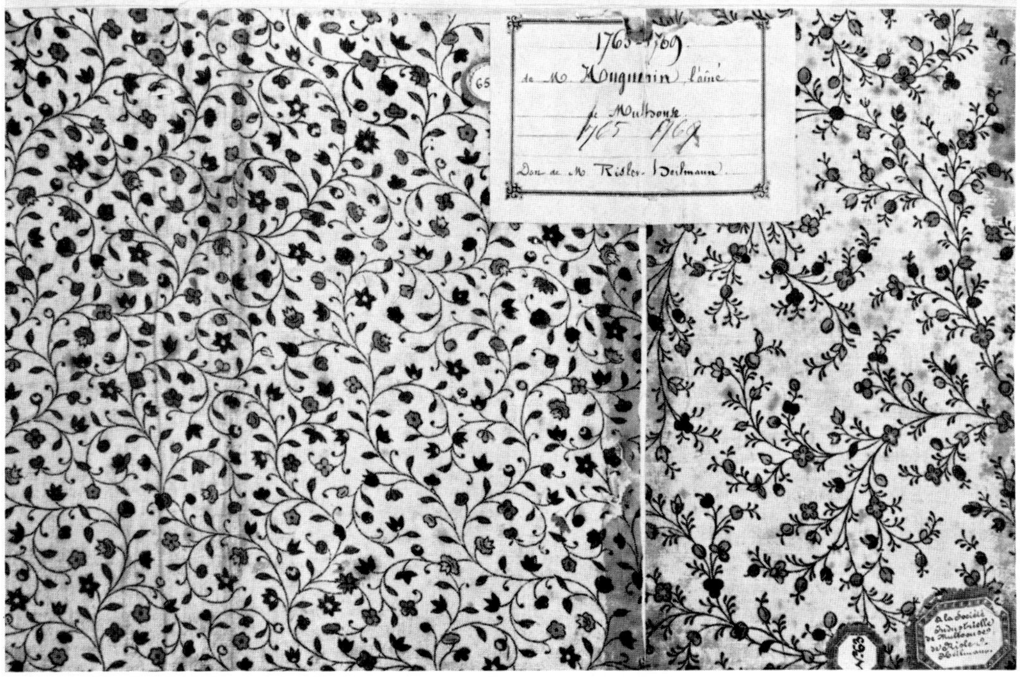

7

Fig. 5/6 By Feer & Huguenin, Mulhouse. 1760

Fig. 7 By Huguenin the Elder, Mulhouse. 1765–1769

Fig. 8   Design signed Haury, made by Schlumberger. May 1779

Fig. 9   Design signed Godinot & Gergonne, 4 January 1780
(Godinot worked for Rissler – probably Nicolas Rissler & Co., Mulhouse & Wesserling)

Fig. 10   By Huguenin, Reber & Co., Mulhouse. 1770

Fig. II   Mulhouse or Munster. c. 1780

Fig. 12   *The Ascension of the Montgolfière*, Mulhouse. 1783

13

14

Fig. 13   By Huguenin the Elder, Mulhouse. 1785

Fig. 14   Heinrich Koechlin, Mulhouse. c. 1785

Fig. 15   By Vetter & Blech, Mulhouse. 1786–1793

Fig. 16   Mulhouse. c. 1790

Fig. 17/18   Linen Sachet (back and front view). Mulhouse. c. 1790

Fig. 19   Bonnet. End 18th century

Fig. 20   Mulhouse. 18th Century

Fig. 21   Border of Table cloth. Alsace, probably Mulhouse. c. 1790

22

23

Fig. 22   Panel. Mulhouse. Probably Jean Koechlin. Late 18th century

Fig. 23   Handkerchief Sachet. Mulhouse. Late 18th century

Fig. 24   Alsace. Probably Jean Hofer & Co. at Mulhouse. Late 18th century

Fig. 25   By Pierre Dollfus & Co, Thann. 1790

Fig. 26   By Royale de Senn & Bidermann, Wesserling. c. 1780 (Style of Pillement)

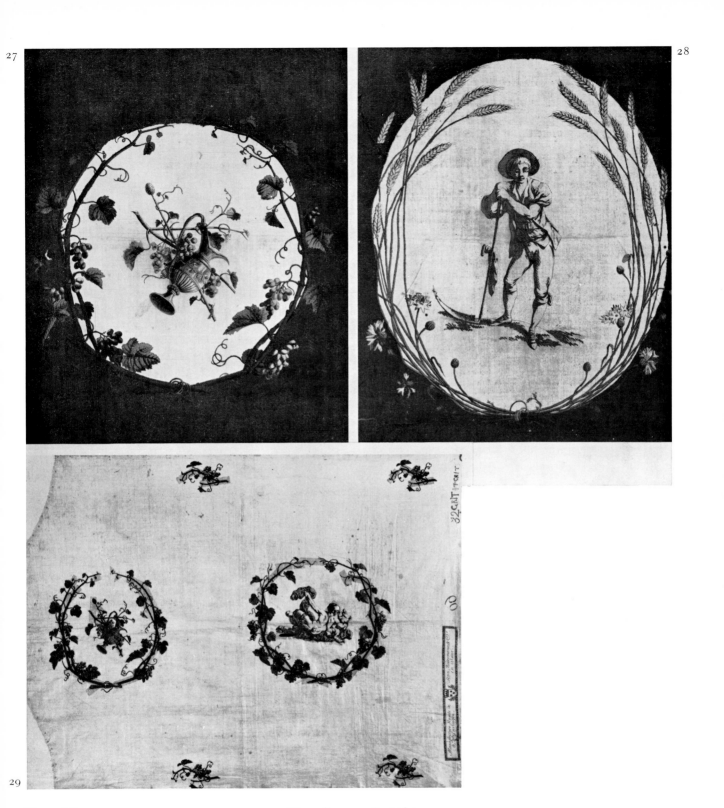

27

28

29

Fig. 27/28   Wesserling. c. 1780–1785

Fig. 29   By Royale de Senn, Bidermann & Co., Wesserling. c. 1785

Fig. 30   Design by Dujardin. Wesserling. c. 1785

Fig. 31/32   Designs by Dujardin. "The Litter" and "The Swing". Wesserling. c. 1785

Fig. 33/34   Designs by Dujardin. "The Halt" and "The Family Rest". Wesserling. c. 1785

36

Fig. 35   By Bidermann, Odier & Co., Wesserling. 1785–1790

Fig. 36   Wesserling. Late 18th or early 19th century

Fig. 37   Cloth woven at Wesserling
and printed by Jean Koechlin at Mulhouse. 1803

Fig. 38   By Haussmann Brothers at Logelbach, near Colmar. 1775–1785

Fig. 39 (top and bottom)   Probably Haussmann Brothers at Logelbach near Colmar.
                            The top example is marked P.W. 1770–1775

40

41

Fig. 40/41 By Haussmann Brothers at Logelbach near Colmar. 1777

43

44

Fig. 42-44   By Haussmann Brothers at Logelbach near Colmar. 1777

Fig. 45/46   By Haussmann Brothers at Logelbach near Colmar. 1777

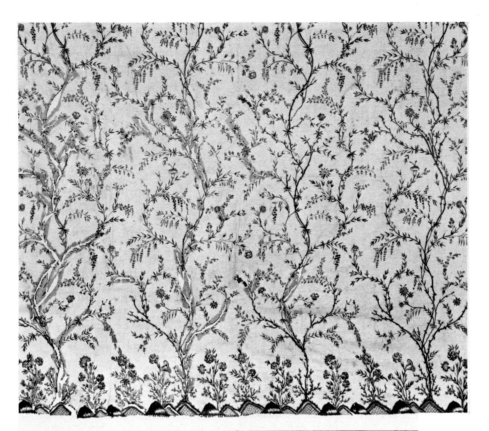

Fig. 47   By Haussmann Brothers at Logelbach near Colmar. 1777–1778
               (Note the resemblance between this and a pezzoto of Genoa)

Fig. 48   By Haussmann Brothers at Logelbach, near Colmar. 1778

Fig. 49   By Haussmann Brothers at Logelbach near Colmar. 1777–1800

Fig. 50   By Haussmann Brothers at Logelbach near Colmar. 1778

Fig. 51/52   By Haussmann Brothers at Logelbach, near Colmar. 1778

Fig. 53/54   By Haussmann Brothers at Logelbach near Colmar. 1779

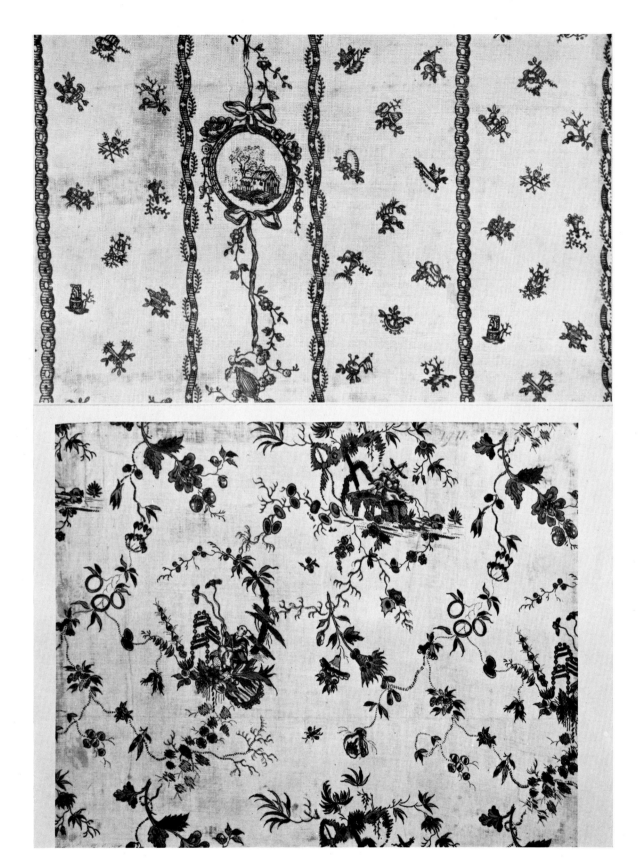

Fig. 55   Alsace. Possibly Haussmann & Brothers at Logelbach. c. 1780

Fig. 56   By Haussmann Brothers at Logelbach, near Colmar. 1780

Fig. 57/58   By Haussmann Brothers at Logelbach near Colmar. 1780

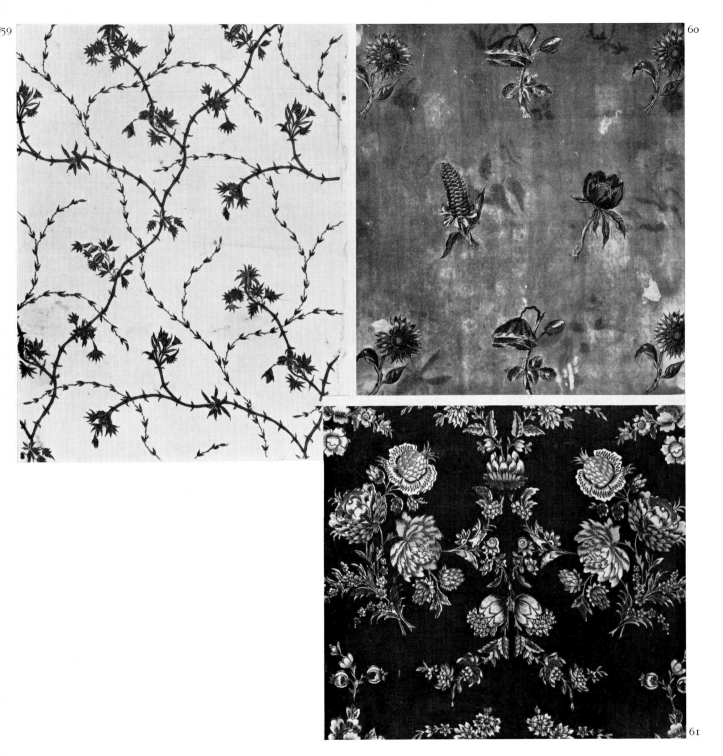

59

60

61

Fig. 59   By Haussmann Brothers at Logelbach near Colmar. 1780

Fig. 60/61   Probably by Haussmann Brothers at Logelbach. c. 1780

62

63

64

Fig. 62-64   By Haussmann Brothers, Logelbach. 1780, 1781 and 1783 respectively

Fig. 65   By Haussmann Brothers at Logelbach near Colmar. 1784

Fig. 66   Alsace. Late 18th century. Probably by Haussmann Brothers at Logelbach

Fig. 67   Design inscribed by Haury & Haury the Elder. Made for Haussmann Brothers. March 1789

Fig. 68   Corner of cloth or Handkerchief. By Haussmann Brothers at Logelbach. c. 1795

Fig. 69   By Haussmann Brothers at Logelbach near Colmar. 1785

Fig. 70   Design by Haury. c. 1796. Members of the Haury family worked for Haussmann Brothers.
A piece of material from this design is in the Musée de l'Impression sur Etoffes, Mulhouse

Fig. 71   Edging by Haussmann Brothers at Logelbach. End 18th century

Fig. 72   Edging by Haussmann Brothers at Logelbach. September 1789

Fig. 73   Handkerchief (part) by Hausmann Brothers, Logelbach. c. 1790

Fig. 74/75   Alsace. Possibly Haussmann Brothers at Logelbach. 18th century

Fig. 76   Possibly Haussmann Brothers at Logelbach. Late 18th century

Fig. 77   By Haussmann Brothers at Logelbach. Late 18th century

Fig. 78   Hartmann manufacture, either Munster founded 1776 by J. J. Schmaltzer Senior,
but which only went under the name of André Hartmann and Henri Riege in 1780,
or Mulhouse under the old name Hartmann & Cie which later became Wolf, Risler & Cie in 1775. 1777

Fig. 79   Manufacture Colmar. 1796

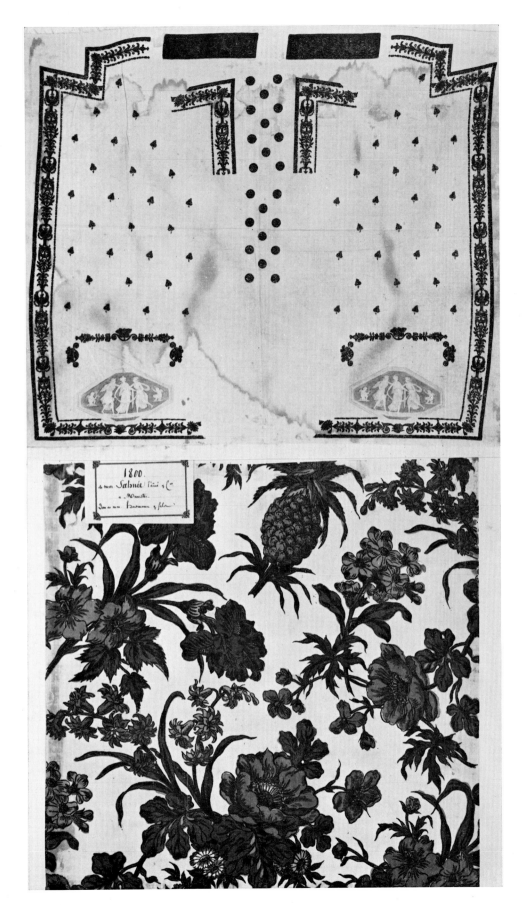

Fig. 80   Printed waistcoat, design by Marie-Bonaventure Lebert,
probably for André Hartmann at Munster. 1796–1800

Fig. 81   By Soehnée the Elder & Cie at Munster. c. 1800

Fig. 82

Alsace. c. 1775

Fig. 83

Design engraved by Lehmann. July 1777

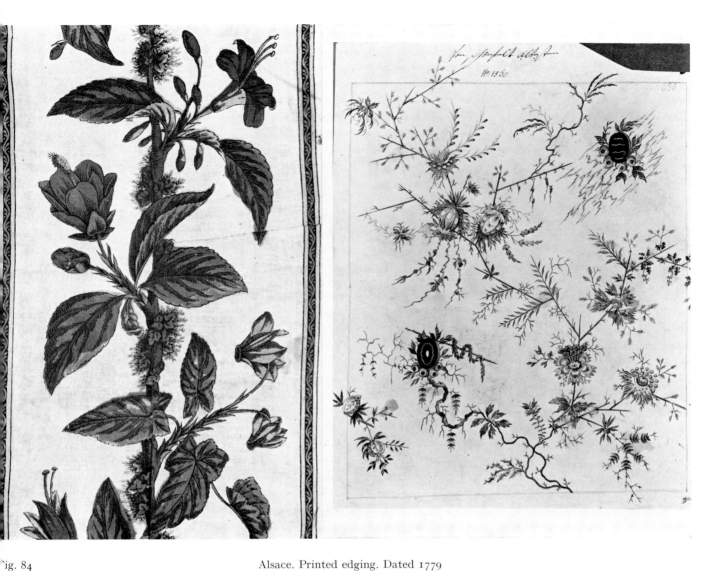

Fig. 84   Alsace. Printed edging. Dated 1779

Fig. 85   Design by Schoenfeld the Elder. c. 1780

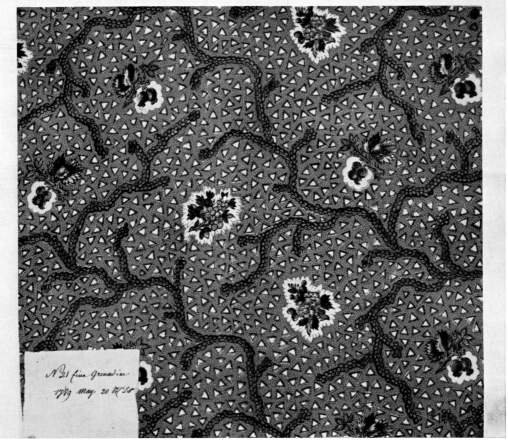

Fig. 86   Alsace. c. 1780

Fig. 87   Alsace. May 20th 1789

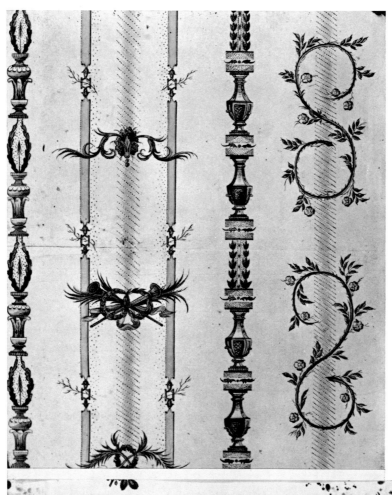

Fig. 88   Design for printing. 1797

Fig. 89   Alsace. c. 1791

Fig. 90   Design for printing. 1797

Fig. 91   Unknown manufacturer. Alsace 18th century

Fig. 92   Design. 1796–1797

Fig. 93   Design by Schoenfeld. 27th January 1797

Fig. 94   Design engraved by H. Dietrich. 18th December 1796

Fig. 95   Design by Lehmann. c.1796

Fig. 96/97   Printed borders. Alsace. 18th century

Fig. 98/99   Alsace. 18th century

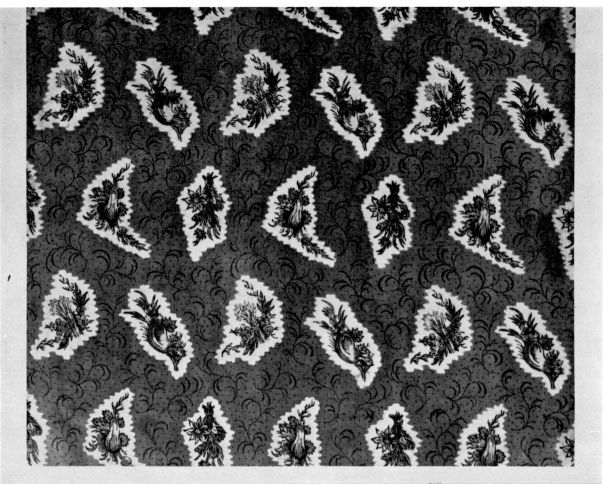

Fig.100/101   Alsace. 18th century

Fig. 102/103   Alsace. 18th century

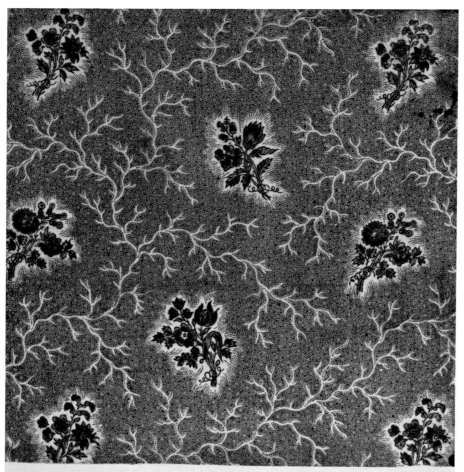

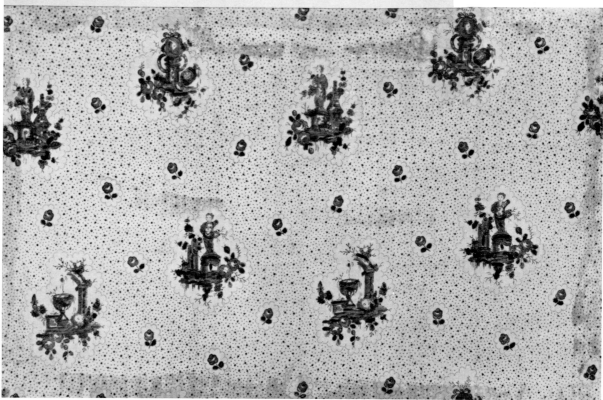

Fig. 104/105   Alsace. 18th century

Fig. 106   Alsace. End 18th century

Fig. 107   Table-cloth (part). Alsace. 18th century

Fig. 108   Alsace. 18th century

Fig. 109/110   Alsace. End 18th century

Fig. 111/112   Alsace. End 18th century

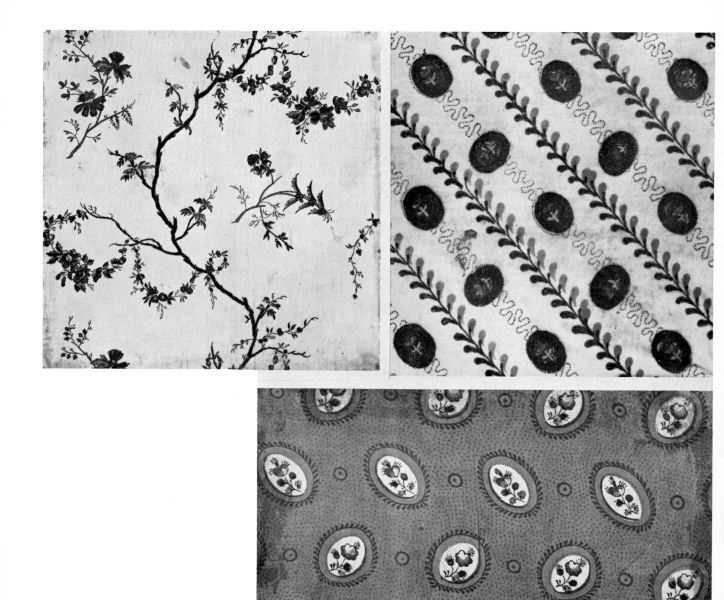

Fig. 113-115   Alsace. End 18th century

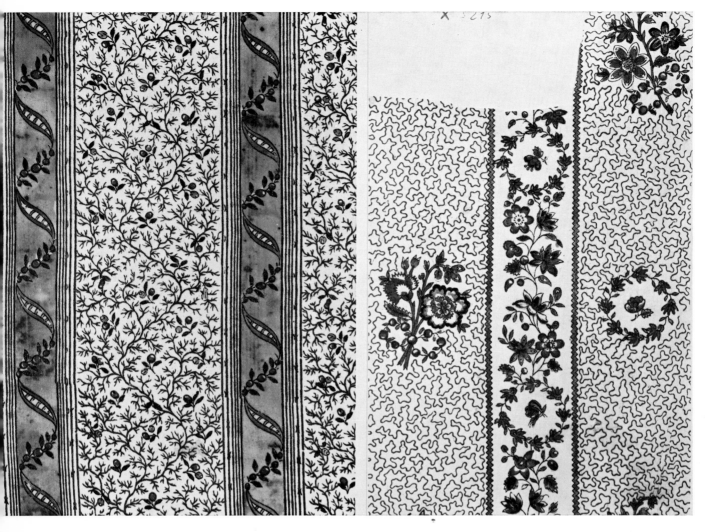

Alsace. End 18th century
(*from the collection* TACO S.A., France)

Fig. 118/119

Alsace. End 18th century
(*from the collection* TACO S.A., France)

Fig. 120-123

Alsace. End 18th century
(*from the collection* TACO S.A., France)